James Swan

A Dissuasion to Great-Britain and the Colonies, from the Slave Trade to Africa

Shewing the contradiction this trade bears, both to laws divine and

provincial

James Swan

A Dissuasion to Great-Britain and the Colonies, from the Slave Trade to Africa
Shewing the contradiction this trade bears, both to laws divine and provincial

ISBN/EAN: 9783337309282

Printed in Europe, USA, Canada, Australia, Japan

Cover: Foto ©ninafisch / pixelio.de

More available books at **www.hansebooks.com**

A

DISSUASION

T O

GREAT-BRITAIN

A N D   T H E

COLONIES,

F R O M   T H E

SLAVE TRADE TO AFRICA.

S H E W I N G,

The Contradiction this Trade bears, both to Laws divine and provincial ; the Difadvantages arifing from it, and Advantages from abolifhing it, both to EUROPE and AFRICA, particularly to BRITAIN and the Plantations.

A L S O   S H E W I N G,

How to put this Trade to AFRICA on a juft and lawful Footing.

By JAMES SWAN,
A Native of GREAT-BRITAIN, and Friend to the Welfare of this CONTINENT.

BOSTON : NE.
Printed by E. RUSSELL, near the New Intelligence-Office and Auction-room, and next the Cornfield, Union-ftreet.

DEDICATION.

To all FRIENDS to LIBERTY.

FELLOW SUBJECTS,

IT is to you I dedicate this Treatise, and beg your protection of the same, hoping it will meet with a kind reception.

THE approbation men of character and sense have given the following Work, has made me venture it into your hands : And I hope in the perusal you will keep in view the Author, I am certain you cannot then fail of making great allowances. I am a *North-Briton !*

Briton ! And when you know that, it alone may be judged by fome, fufficient to brand me with the hateful name of *Tory*, and thereby condemn this Diffuafion. But let me inform you (for there is no general rule without an exception) that I am a moft fincere well-wifher to the common caufe of *Liberty*, both *perfonal* and *conftitutional* ; then you will, give me a place in the lift of your ftaunch Friends, and accept of this Attempt, as intended to be a mean of abolifhing one great part of *Slavery* here.

If there is any merit in endeavouring to fet free from *Bondage* our fellow creatures, and in trying to promote the good and welfare of any nation, province, country,

or

or individual, furely I may claim it; for my fincere endeavour is to thefe purpofes: And if I fhould happen to mifs my aim, I fhall fit down fatisfied with the merit of a good intent.

READERS, I have but one favour to afk of you, which is, to perufe this Performance with an open unbiaffed mind; overlooking any defects you may obferve in thefe fheets, knowing they are the hafty and undigefted thoughts of the Author, put together with more good intent than ability; after this you may either reject or practife, according to your own confciences, and the light of this Treatife, if there is any to be found in it. *Enflaving* your fellow men, and ufing and maffacring them as they do in the
Weft-

Weſt-Indies and Southern Provinces, is a matter of too great importance to be only ſlightly thought of. And as I hope you have the *humanity* of *Britons*, and that *love of Liberty*, with which every true *Engliſhman* is, or ought to be poſſeſſed of, you will not countenance it, but declare yourſelves as I do, *well-wiſhers of the Britiſh Empire, and conſequently enemies to* Slavery.

Accept then, Friends and Brethren in one common cauſe, this ſmall token of that love and veneration which I bear to freedom, (for no country can be called free where there is one Slave) and give me leave to ſubſcribe myſelf,

Your Friend and

humble Servant,

JAMES SWAN.

THE

PREFACE.

I HAD not well arrived in *America*, when casting my eyes on so many Black Slaves, I immediately found a warm inclination arise in my breast, to do my endeavours for relieving them by publishing to the world my sentiments upon their state.

SCARCE

Scarce had I time to draw a breath of this air, before I immediately applied myfelf to enquire into the ftate of this *Slavery*, and the conftitution upon which it is founded, and having met with proper preliminaries by way of foundation for a fmall Treatife, I fet myfelf to work in forming, and in fhort finifhed this Pamphlet.

From the confideration of the fmallnefs of this production, and my inability to treat the fubject properly, I was nigh refolving not to prefix my name hereto : But thinking again, fome oppofite party might take hold of that, I thought it moft proper to fhew my common fignature, knowing the

the caufe I defend is good and well founded.

Some will no doubt be furprifed that I have wrote this Diffuafion after the form of a Sermon : It is eafily accounted for. A Sermon being *a difcourfe of inftruction pronounced by a Divine for the edification of the people.* I am no Divine nor ever expect to be ; but I hope that is no reafon why thefe fheets fhould not be of publick benefit, as my defign was for that end ; I chofe to write it in this form, as being the trueft way to difplay with perfpicuity and plainnefs the unlawfulnefs, &c. of the Slave Trade, for which purpofe I have attempted it in different heads and branches, in fome of which

are

are contained many pertinent re-
marks or obfervations on this inhuman Commerce; and I thought
further, it was the eafieft method
for myfelf, and plaineft for my
Readers; it being intended for the
weakeft and higheft capacities.

It may be objected by fome, that
the writings on this fubject are too
numerous already. I anfwer, that
however many there may be ex-
tant, (although I could find but very
few) yet there are none fo full as
not to admit of amendments or
improvements : If fo, and that
thefe may not altogether be
of inconfiderable ufe to mankind, why may not I make them ?
and why may they not be tranf-
mitted to mankind ?

A

A Treatise of this kind may not be unneceſſary, notwithſtanding many Books, Pamphlets, and Letters have been publiſhed on the ſubject.

But however ineffectual this Treatiſe may prove hereafter a-mong men, this I comfort myſelf with, it is as full, conſidering the largeneſs, as any upon the ſub-ject which I have ſeen ; and there are few arguments that poſſibly could be advanced, or citations drawn from Scripture concerning man-ſelling, &c. that have eſcaped, in trying to wean men from this baſe and inhuman trade. And in fine, if this Work meets with encou-ragement equal to the Author's care and endeavours to make it

the

the moſt uſeful of the kind, by having the deſired effect he ſhall eſteem himſelf ſufficiently re-warded.

Wɪтн regard to the Diſſuaſion, I leave the Reader to judge, after having read it over cooly and im-partially, whether it ought to be approved or diſapproved ; if the former, it will no doubt meet with his protection in publick. But I have ſomething to aſk, which I beg may not be refuſed, and that is, if you have not a fund of pa-tience laid up in ſtore, before you begin to peruſe it, you are requeſt-ed to lay it aſide, until you have.

Tнеʀе is one ſmall part of it taken from *Poſtlethwayt*'s Dictio-nary

nary of Commerce. Another part from *A. Benezett*'s **Caution** to *Great-Britain* and her **Colonies,** both which Authors I am very glad were born before me, they having affifted me fo far. And with regard to the remaining **part,** I can tell where it came from.

As it is neceffary in order **to** bring about a change in any, par- ticularly a publick affair, to touch the minds of the people with a juft and true fenfe of the unlaw- fulnefs of the thing wanted to **be** removed, that to the end they may be unanimous in the abo- lifhment thereof ; this Diffua- fion I am convinced you will **find** upon perufal, is calculated **for** that purpofe, and am very fenfi-
ble

xvi   P R E F A C E.

ble, that it alone never can ſtrike
the great blow without the legiſ-
lative force added to it.

I WILL detain you no longer ;
indeed I have almoſt run into an
Introduction amidſt this Preface :
But it could not well be other-
wiſe, the connexion between
them was ſo great, and had I ſe-
parated them, I ſhonld have in-
curred your diſpleaſure, by in-
creaſing the Prolegomenas to a
degree larger than the Diſſuaſion
itſelf.

J. S.

DISSUASION, &c.

THE fubject of which thefe few fheets treat, would have been one of the laft I fhould have ventured upon; had not the delufion of the men who are concerned in enflaving the people, called *Negroes* appeared fo glaring, and the contradiction that the *Slave Trade* bears to Chriftianity, prompted me to it.

I SHALL be as cool and impartial in treating of this matter, as any Britifh fubject or Chriftian can : But why do I fay cool ? It is impoffible I fhould fpeak cooly of fuch bafe, unchriftan, and inhuman practices, in a land of Liberty and Chriftianity : However, in cafe any thing fhould be mentioned in the fequel that may give unintended offence to any perfon, I hope the tender feelings for thefe diftreffed Captives, with which I am poffeffed, and the warmth that is in my breaft, to have this Trade abolifhed, will be fufficient excufe.

I PROPOSE dividing the following Treatife into thefe different heads.   I,

I. SHEW, that this cuftom of making Slaves of our fellow-men, is expreffly againft the revealed laws of God.

II. THAT it is likewife againft the law of nature, and the Charter of this Province.

III. The difadvantages arifing from this bafe Trade.

IV. THE advantages arifing from abolifhing it. And,

V. CONCLUDE with a fhort admonition to thófe concerned, and a method to put the Trade to *Africa* on a juft and lawful footing.

THE firft head was, That the cuftom óf making Slaves of our fellow creatures, is expreffly againft the revealed laws of GOD. And in treating of this part, I fhall divide it into the following branches. 1ft. By the laws of GOD, *He that ftealeth and felleth a man, fhall be put to death.* 2d. *He in whofe hands he fhall be found, fhall be put to death,* by the fame laws. 3d. *He that buyeth a Servant and ferveth him fix years, fhall fet him free the feventh, and furnifh him liberally with what he hath.* And 4th. *If thy Brother,* that is, your fellow-creature, *be fold unto*

unto thee, thou shall not compel him to serve as a Bond-man ; but as an hired Servant.

THE firſt branch under this head is, *He that ſtealeth and ſelleth a man, ſhall be put to death.* This is one of the moſt expreſs laws of *Moſes*, as you may ſee in *Exod.* xxi. 16, two firſt, and laſt clauſes of the verſe, there mentioned in the moſt peremptory words ; *And he that ſtealeth a man, and ſelleth him, ſhall ſurely be put to death.* It certainly can be looked upon in no other light in the Merchants and Ship-maſters who are in this Trade to *Africa,* than ſtealing of men, being acceſſary to, and aiding in inciting them to war one with another, and for this purpoſe, ſupplying them with prodigious quantities of arms and ammunition, whereby they are hurried into confuſion, bloodſhed, and all the extremities of temporal miſery, which muſt conſequently beget in their minds ſuch a general deteſtation and ſcorn of the Chriſtian name, as may deeply affect, if not wholly preclude, their belief of the great truths of our holy religion. Thus an inſatiable deſire of gain prevails with their Kings, who, inſtead of being protectors of their people, for this alluring

bait

bait laid before them, by the *European* and *American* Factors, or Ship-masters, invade the Liberties of thefe unhappy people, and occafion their opreffion. Thefe Kings, whenever they want goods fend to the Ship-masters, acquainting them they have Negroes, and fometimes the Factors and Ship-masters fend to acquaint them, that they have a quantity of goods, and want Slaves for the fame. Thefe Chiefs, whether they have Slaves then or not, agree, and immediately go to war with their neighbours, and in procuring three or four hundred prifoners, burn five or fix towns, as appears by the following extract from a Surgeon's Journal in a *Liverpool* veffel,

Seftro, December 29, 1724.

" N O trade to-day, though many
" Traders came on board ; they inform
" us, that the people are gone to war
" within land, and will bring pri-
" foners enough in two or three days ;
" in hopes of which we ftay.

" 30th. No trade yet ; but our Traders
" came on board to-day and informed us
" the people had burnt four towns, fo
" that to-morrow we expect Slaves off.

" 31ft. FAIR weather, but no trade yet;
we

" we fee each night towns burning ; but
" we hear the *Seftro* men are many of them
" killed by the inland Negroes, fo that
" we fear this war will be unfuccefsful.

" THE 2d of *January*. Laft night
" we faw a prodigious fire break out
" about eleven o'clock, and this morn-
" ing faw the town of *Seftro* burnt down
" to the ground, (it contained fome
" hundred houfes) fo that we find their
" enemies are too hard for them at pre-
" fent; confequently our trade fpoiled
" here, fo that about feven o'clock we
" weighed anchor, as did alfo the three
" other veffels, to proceed lower down."

HERE follows another relation taken
from an original Journal of a Surgeon
who failed out of *New-York*, " Being
" on the Coaft of *Guinea* at a place
" called *Bafalia*, the Commander of the
" veffel, according to cuftom, fent a
" perfon on fhore, with a prefent to the
" King, acquainting him with his
" arrival, and informing him they
" wanted a cargo of Slaves. The
" King promifed to furnifh them, and
" in order to do it, fet out to war
" againft his enemies ; defigning alfo
" to furprife fome town, and take all
the

" the people prisoners : Some time af-
" ter, the King sent them word, he had
" not yet met with the desired success,
" having been twice repulsed in at-
" tempting to break up two towns ;
" but that he still hoped to procure a
" number of Slaves for them, and in
" this design persisted, until he met his
" enemies in the field, where a battle was
" fought, which lasted three days, dur-
" ing which time, the engagement was
" so bloody that four thousand five hun-
" dred men were slain on the spot. Think
" (says he) what a pitiful fight it was
" to see the Widows weeping over their
" lost Husbands, Orphans deploring the
" loss of their Fathers, &c." Oh ! shock-
ing spectacles ! to see four or five towns
burnt, and four thousand five hundred
people killed, for the sake of taking three
or four hundred, and you ! you ! Merchants, Ship-masters and Factors the cause
of it all ! Think you ever to get the crime
of spilling so much blood repented of ?

It is a known custom among the Factors who reside in *Africa,* and the Ship-
masters who trade there, to corrupt
many Negroes on the sea coast, who
stop at no act of cruelty for gain. They
make

make it a practice, to steal abundance of
little Blacks of both sexes, when found
on the roads, or in the fields, where
their Parents keep them all day to watch
the corn, &c. Can it be denied that the
Africans are *stolen* after so many proofs of
it, and if it is not direct stealth in the Ship-
masters, &c. yet it is the same in effect ;
for if they did not go there and en-
tice the Chiefs with money or goods,
there would be no wars, as is the case at
present ; and there would be none stolen
if the stealers were not bribed by the Factors or Ship-masters ; and not only those
that are made Slaves of, there would still
be ten thousand others who are killed in
the broils, that would be saved, were they
to discontinue this base Trade.

Thus far I have shewn that they are
stolen. They may say they pay for them.
I answer, they give money or goods by
way of price to some of the Princes and
Negroes, who, for the sake of lucre,
take them prisoners by war or stealth, so
that what money they give these scoun-
drels, (forgive me the expression ; for,
what name can a man expect who would
take his Father or Brother and sell them
for gain ?) who take them in these ways
cannot

cannot be looked upon as a price paid in lieu, for the Negroes themfelves never condefcend to be mancipated, as they get none of the money that is pretendedly given for them. They at length arrive at the port, the Ship-mafter fell them at a moft exorbitant profit, and in a few voyages he makes what he calls his fortune ; this is all he aimed at and wifhed for ; and what follows, fecures his eternal deftruction, unlefs timely repented of : For the truth of this, I could mention very ftriking inftances of men, who I fee almoft every day ; but I do not chufe mentioning names, for fear of feeing them contemned and defpifed by every well thinking perfon.

I need add no more on this branch, it being clear that they are ftolen in every fenfe it can be taken ; they, the Shipmafters, &c. being the fole caufe of the many wars and broils that are amongft the Negro Princes and Chiefs, confequently the caufe of thefe poor creatures being taken and made Slaves of, and of the many thoufands that are killed in the wars : Befides, it is not, nor can be denied that they fell them, fo that they who practife this branch of Man-ftealing

ing and felling can expect nothing but
the penalties of God's laws, which he,
in his own time, will inflict, since man!
indolent man! will not punish them with
death, as warranted sufficiently by the
above cited passage in holy writ.

Before I leave this branch it may
not be improper to give my Readers a
short sketch of the barbarous usage these
unhappy people meet with from the
Ship-masters in their passage from *Africa*. After they have got them on board
shackled two and two together, they keep
them confined below all the passage, never permitting more than two on deck at
a time to take one breath of fresh air,
the most common blessing we enjoy,
conscious that they are doing wrong to
these people, and not certain but God
might raise them against the Ship-master
and his crew, if they had the least opportunity to stir up an insurrection in the
ship, to retrieve their Liberty which
they had in their own country, and which
they ought to enjoy by the laws of God,
of *Britain*, and the Plantations.

For the Reader's true satisfaction as to
this inhuman and unchristian usage,
which could be expected of no other
D than

than Barbarians, I fhall here narrate fome
accounts which have been given by men
concerned ni the Slave Trade.

First, the following cafe is mentioned in *Aftley*'s Collection of Voyages, by
John Atkins, Surgeon on board Admiral
Ogle's fquadron, " Of one *Harding*, Maf-
" ter of a veffel, in which feveral of the
" Men-flaves and a Woman-flave had
" attempted to rife in order to recover
" their Liberty ; fome of whom the
" Mafter of his own authority fentenced
" to cruel deaths, making them firft eat
" the hearts and liver of one of thofe he
" killed. The woman he hoifted by
" the thumbs, whiped, and flafhed with
" knives before other Slaves, until fhe
" died." Oh unparralelled cruelty !

Next is an account given by a Ship-
mafter who brought a Cargo of Slaves
to *Barbadoes*, upon an enquiry what had
been the fuccefs of the voyage, he anfwered, " That he had found it a difficult
" matter to fet the Negroes a fighting
" with each other in order to procure
" the number he wanted." This fhews,
Reader, what methods they practife to
obtain thefe Slaves, *by fetting them a fighting with each other.* " But when he had
                                " obtained

" obtained his end, having filled his
" veffel withSlaves, a new difficulty arofe
" from their refufal to take food : Thofe
" defperate creatures chufing rather to
" die with hunger than to be carried from
" their native country." Upon a further
enquiry how he got them to forego this
defperate refolution, he anfwered, "That
" he obliged all theNegroes to come on
" deck, where they perfifting in their
" refolution of not taking food, he cau-
" fed his failors to lay hold on one of the
" moft obftinate, who chopped the poor
" creature into fmall pieces, forcing fome
" of the others to eat a part of the man-
" gled body ; fwearing to the furvivors,
" that he would ufe them all one after
" the other in the fame manner if they
" did not confent to eat." This horrid
execution he applauded as a good act,
it having had the defired effect in cau-
fing them to take food.

" As deteftable and fhocking as thefe
ufages to the poor Negroes may appear to
fuch whofe hearts are not yet hardened
by the practife of that cruelty which the
love of wealth by degrees introduceth into the human mind, it will not be ftrange
to thofe who have been concerned or employed in the Trade."   THE

THE fecond branch was, *If he be found in his hands, he furely fhall be put to death.* This is the third and fourth claufe of the before cited verfe in *Exod. If he be found in his hands.* This is to be underftood in two fenfes, either found in the Ship-mafter's hands who ftole him, or bought, as he fays, or in the perfon's hands who purchafes him. As to the firft of thefe fenfes in which this paffage may be taken, if the laws of GOD, yea, even of man, were to be put into execution, he, the ftealer, or even the buyer, would be punifhed with death, for it is clear as to Man-ftealing, that it deferves death, by the above paffage of Scripture, and it is no lefs with regard to buying : But why do I fay buying ? For no money can be equal to the worth of a man : Buying, I admit that word becaufe Ship-mafters and others in this Trade, fay, for their juftification that they purchafed the Negroes, but as there are no laws, either of GOD or man, for the buying and ftealing of *Africans*, I am inclined to think it cannot be fuppofed, but they juftly deferve death. And in the fecond fenfe, the man who buys the *Africans* or Negroes is full as culpable as the ftealer, and liable to the fame punifh-

punishment, for Scripture does not point out particularly either of them, but only just, *If he be found in his hands,* that is, in any man's hands, so that it can be proved he stole or bought him, *he surely shall be put to death.*

THE third part was, *He that buyeth a Servant and serveth him six years, shall set him free the seventh, and furnish him liberally with what he hath.* The first part of this branch is proved in three different texts, *viz. Exod.* xxi. 2. *Deut.* xv. 12. and *Jer.* xxxiv. 14. In all which parts it is expressly mentioned, *That if an* Hebrew *Servant be sold unto thee,* or if you buy him he *shall serve thee six years, and the seventh, thou shall let him go free from thee,* that is, he shall pay nothing for his Liberty.

SOME persons for argument sake may object to this, saying, these people are not *Hebrews,* as mentioned in these texts of Scripture, but *Heathens.* This may be difficult enough to determine. However, admit they are *Heathens,* (although it is well known they are not) it must be owned by those who know them, that the natives of *Africa* have exalted notions of a Deity. It is an odd method these
Traders

Traders take to civilize and teach them the Chriſtian religion, by importing one hundred thouſand of them yearly into *Virginia* and other Southern Provinces, together with the *Weſt-India* iſlands, where they are kept in greater darkneſs than before, as they are not allowed to worſhip GOD on the Sabbath ; but are employed in worldly buſineſs on that day, which is a ſcandal to the Rulers of the *Britiſh* Colonies and Iſlands where ſuch things are practiſed. It is ſubverſive of the Chriſtian religion not to allow thoſe ignorant people the benefit of it, who make up more than two thirds of the inhabitants of the beforementioned places. It is expreſſly againſt the laws of GOD ; for he gave *Paul* and other Apoſtles commiſſion to go and preach the goſpel to every nation, kindred, and tongue ; but inſtead of that, where the goſpel is preached throughout the *Britiſh* Colonies, and where theſe people might expect to receive the light of it ; I ſay, inſtead of that, they are kept from divine worſhip on Sundays, and never once in their lifetime admitted to church, but obliged to cultivate their ſmall piece of ground allowed them by their Maſters.

THE laſt part of the verſe runs thus,
And

And shall furnish him liberally with what he hath. That is, when the Servant hath served thee six years, as expressed in *Exod.* xxi. 2, and *Deut.* xv. 12. *Then in the seventh year you shall let him go free from you* ; and in ver. 13. *Thou shall not let him go away empty.* Ver. 14. *Thou shall furnish him liberally out of thy flock, and out of thy floor, and out of thy wine press* ; *of that wherewith the* LORD *thy* GOD *hath blessed thee, thou shalt give him. This is in token that thou dost acknowledge the benefit that thou hast received by his labours.* Marg. Bible.

IT is still further required to set your Servants or Bond-men free at the above appointed time, by the 15th verse of the same chap. *And thou shalt remember that thou wast a Bond-man in the land of* Egygt, *and the* LORD *thy* GOD *redeemed thee* ; *therefore I command thee this thing to day. I command thee.* You are ordered, yea, commanded to do *this thing.* What thing? To set free your Bond-servants after six years service. You are commanded to do it *to day, viz.* At the expiration of six years, for, says GOD, by the voice of his Servant, *I command thee this thing to day.*

THERE is a blessing promised to those who do this thing in ver. 18 of the above chap.

chap. After enjoining that it may not feem hard unto you in fending away this Servant, as he hath been worth a double hired one, in ferving thee fix years, he fays, *and the* LORD *thy* GOD *fhall blefs thee in all that thou doeft.* Sweet encouragement for poor finful fouls! To be blefled in every thing that they do. What man will forfeit this great blefling for the fake of the fervice of one, two, or more Servants for life? Will he allow himfelf to be curfed by GOD in every thing that he doeth for the fmall gain he can make by their fervices? This charming promife of a blefling in all that thou doeft, and the dreadful events that may take place in contradicting the command of GOD, I hope will make fuch impreflions upon the minds of men, that they will not bind Servant to ferve above fix years; but will fet him at liberty in the feventh year, and give him liberally of what the LORD hath blefled them with, as required in the above cited text. If you think you have not enough of this, pafs along to

THE fourth and laft fection on this head, *If thy Brother be fold unto thee, thou fhall not compel him to ferve as a Bond-man; but as an hired Servant.* This is proved by *Lev.* xxv. 39, 40. where it is faid, *If thy Brother*

Brother that dwelleth by thee be waxen poor,
and be fold unto thee, thou fhalt not compel
him to ferve as a Bond-fervant. This is
expreffly againft making Slaves of any
of our poor Brethren, or compeling them
to ferve as Bond-fervants. *If thy Bro-*
ther that dwelleth by thee be waxen poor, are
the words of the verfe ; the poor *Afri-*
cans who fall into the hands of the Men-
wolves that prowl on their coafts, are obliged to ferve their lifetime, and their children after them : This is being Bond-men
with a witnefs, and as we have great reafon to believe they are poor enough when
they fteal them, they are kept fo forever
after, not having means to make a penny
themfelves. The *Africans* will be underftood,
if not primarily intended, to be the people
mentioned in this text ! It is faid, *Thy Brother*
who dwelleth by thee : When they are in *Afri-*
ca it is certain they are at a great diftance ;
but when they come to *America* or the *Weft-*
Indies they then dwell *by us ;* therefore I think,
from the above citations, no perfon can buy
thefe people, and oblige them and their
children to ferve as Slaves, without incur-
ing the difpleafure of GOD and his punifhments for difobeying his juft commands.

IT may be added, as in v. 42d of the fame
chap. *For they are my fervants, which I brought*
E   *forth*

forth out of Eygpt ; *they shall not be sold as Bond-men.* The last part of this verse is expressly against *selling* them as Bond-men. Should it be objected, that the *Africans* were not *brought forth out of the land of* Egypt, it would not affect the controversy. I would sincerely advise every man who is in this abominable Trade not to persist in it, seeing the many threats and commands against him in GOD's laws, and the blessings that are promised if he does not.

THE IId General Head proposed, is, That this practice of making Slaves of our Brethren is likewise against the law of nature, and the Charter of this Province. The first part of this head, may be easily proved by the following texts of Scripture ; *Matt.* vii. 12. *Therefore all things whatsoever ye would that men should do to you, do ye even so to them.* *Luke* vi. 31. *And as you would that men should do to you, do ye so to them likewise.* Who is that proud one that will not receive these instructions ? And who is that man that will do unto any person, either white or black, Christian or Savage, contrary to what he would that he should do to him ? This would be acting contrary to reason and common sense. Would any person consent to have himself torn from his friends and native country, and be

made

made a Slave for life, and to have his dear, dear little children continue in the fame condition from one generation to another ? No ; furely no perfon would agree to that. Well then, it certainly muft be contrary to the laws of nature, chriftianity, and fub-verfive of the texts juft quoted, which were wrote for our direction and guidance in this world. It is likewife certain, that thofe who carry on this Trade, do not unto men as they would men fhould do to them ; for if thefe poor people which they, the Ship-mafters take from their own Country and then fell for Slaves, were doing to them as they are done to, they would (were it in their power, which feldom is the cafe, the owners being confcious of the wrong they are doing, and dreading what naturally would follow) revenge the injury they re-ceive in being made Slaves, and refume that Liberty again, which was wrongful-ly taken from them ; I fay, they would often revenge the injury offered them by killing the Captain of the fhip who had taken them to be mancipated for life, and would ferve in the fame manner the Owners of the veffel if they could get them, who are no better than the Mafters, in putting them into fuch employ. Who could find fault with them ? No perfon. They were only

retrieving

retrieving the moſt common bleſſing we enjoy, Liberty, and inſtead of being puniſhed, the law would protect them in ſo noble an action. But,

READERS, before I leave this, let me beg you to "bring the matter home to your-ſelves, and think whether any condition in life can be more completely miſerable than that of thoſe diſtreſſed Captives. On reflecting, that each of them had ſome ten-der attachments which were broke by the cruel ſeparation! Some Parent or Wife who had not an opportunity of mingling tears in a parting embrace! Perhaps ſome In-fant or aged Parent whom his labour was to feed, and vigilance protect! and him-ſelf under the dreadful apprehenſions of perpetual Slavery."

To inforce this part of the head, allow me, Reader, to intrude a little upon your time, by giving you a ſhort account of the barbarous uſage theſe poor Negroes meet with from their Maſters in the *Weſt-Indies* and Southern Provinces of *North-America*; on reading of which, you will not be long in concluding, that they do not in this caſe obſerve the golden rule.

THE crimes attending the Slave Trade are
greatly

greatly aggravated by the extreme cruel
ufage the Negroes meet with in the Plantations, as well with regard to food and cloathing as the hard and unreafonable
labour that is exacted from them, and what
cannot be forgot, the fevere chaftifements
they frequently fuffer, which is bounded
by the wrath and pleafure of their hard
tafk-mafters. 1ft. As to their food. In *Barbadoes,&c.* * "three quarts of corn and three
herrings are a weeks allowance for a work-
ing Slave; and it is mentioned in theSyftem
of Geography, that in *Jamaica* the Owners
of theNegroSlaves fet afide for each, a piece
of ground, and allow themSundays to cultivate it, the produce of which with a few
falt herrings or other falt fifh is all that is
allowed for their fupport. But need I
go

* It is fuppofed eighty thoufand Negroes, are upon the
Ifland of *Barbadoes*, and yet through the hard labour they
exact of thefe poor creatures, and what of them are killed
through their barbarous chaftifements,a decreafe is made of
five thoufand Slaves yearly, which they are refupplied with
from *Africa*; and it may be reafonably expected, that
the children eighty thoufand Negroes would have, were
they worked in the fame manner with the white people,and
did not fo many of them die through hard labour, and
from the treatment they fuffer: I fay, it may be expected,there would be an increafe of ten thoufand at a mo-
derate computation yearly, inftead of five thoufand decrea-
fing. One may form an idea from this, of what an additi-
onal fupply moft of the *Weft-India* Iflands and Southern
Provinces need, for there is not one of them but what
import a confiderable number of Slaves annually, to
keep up their common ftock.

go fo far as *Jamaica* to prove this ? No. In *Virginia* they do the fame. 2d. As to their cloathing. In theIflands,the allowance for a Slave's cloathing is feldom more than fix yards of oznabrigs a year, and in the Southern Colonies, where the piercing wefterly winds are long and fenfibly felt, thefe poor *Africans* fuffer much for the want of fufficient cloathing; indeed, fhocking to relate ! fome of them are obliged to work moft of the night in boiling-houfes, notwithftanding the hard days work they have performed. TheirOwners make great gain by their Slave's labour. They lay heavy burdens on them, and yet feed and cloath them very fparingly, and fome fcarcely at all; fo that it cannot be wondered that thefe poor creatures are obliged to fhift for their living as they do,which occafions many of them being killed in ftealing potatoes or other food to fatisfy hunger. If they are detected in taking any thing from the plantation they belong to, which they have fo hardly laboured for, they are cruely whiped." Laftly. With refpect to the beating which thefe poor people meet with in the *Weft-Indies.* For the leaft fault they whip them moft unmercifully, *viz.* for not being at work in half an hour after the ufual notice ; fpeaking a word which the Over-

feer may think faucy ; not fhewing refpect
enough to him ; not doing with agility
fome hard piece of work ordered them ;
and any thing which the Overfeer may take
exception at. They beat them with thick
clubs, and you may fee their bodies all wha-
led in a terrible manner.

Mr. *George Whitefield* writes in a letter to
the Planters in *Virginia, Carolina, &c.* " The
" tafk-mafters, by their inhuman ufage and
" unrelenting fcourges have ploughed their
" backs and made long furrows, and at length
" brought them even to death." This is the
fate which great numbers in the iflands and
Southern Provinces meet with. When fpeaking of their cloathing and food, he adds,
" When pafling along, I have viewed your
" plantations cleared and cultivated, many
" fpacious houfes built, and the Owners
" of them faring fumptuoufly every day.
" My blood has frequently run cold with-
" in me to confider how many of your Slaves
" had neither convenient food to eat or
" proper raiment to put on, notwithftand-
" ing many of the comforts you enjoy were
" folely owing to their indefatigable la-
" bours." In *Virginia, &c.* in cafe a Negro gives the flighteft affront to a white
perfon, he goes to the Negroe's Mafter
and

and demands fatisfaction, the Mafter deli-
vers him to the white perfon to take what
fatisfaction he pleafes ; who whips him,
ftrikes him with clubs, and, as is often done,
cuts off his ears, and mark him by cuting
his face, or other parts of his body. What
more could be done to a brute beaft, who
was brought up and defigned for the yoke ?
Oh ! how long will you continue in this
delufion and horrid abufe of the prin-
cipal workmanfhip of God. It is afto-
nifhing how a people who fo much
value themfelves upon their Freedom can
continue in the practice of fo much oppreffion. Will not the groans of this afflicted and
miferable people reach Heaven ! And when
the cup of inequity is filled, the unavoid-
able tendency muft be the pouring forth of
God's judgments upon their oppreffors.
But alas ! is it not too plain that this cruelty has already been the object of divine
anger ? For what greater judgment can
befal any perfon than to become a prey
to that obduracy of heart, that neglectful-
nefs of God, and a calloufnefs to every re-
ligious impreffion ?

I could fay a great deal more concerning the unparralleled cruelty that thefe
Negroes meet with : But I apprehend more
has been faid already than will be believed,
                                    although

although it is far from coming up to the real truth ; for it is impossible my pen can represent in proper colours the hard usage they meet with. The sympathizing Reader must feel the rest, for I can assist him no farther. I believe there are but few that have not heard or read of the cruel treatment of those unhappy mortals. Indeed it is almost incredible that such cruelty should be practised in any of the *British* dominions.

I COULD have quoted a dozen Authors, setting forth the inhuman punishments inflicted upon the *Africans* ; but that would have swelled my page. I hope this short, but true narrative, for great part of which I am much obliged to Mr. *Benezet,* will answer the same end of raising in every breast an utter detestation and abhorrence of the horrid customs and savage usage in the Islands and Colonies abovementioned, and I make no doubt but every one will clearly see, *they do not to these Negroes as they would that they should do to them.*

I THINK it is time to leave this part and go to the last, *viz.* That this base custom is likewise against the Charter of this Province ; as is clearly and most simply demonstrated by a clause in said Charter, granted by King *William* and Queen *Mary,* dated

F

at *Weſtminſter*, the 7th of *October*, in the third year of their reign, wherein, *inter alia*, it is eſtabliſhed and ordained, *That all and every of theSubjects of Us, our Heirs, and Succeſſors, which ſhall go to and inhabit withinOur ſaid Province and territory, and every of their Children which ſhall happen to be born there,or on the ſeas in going thither, or returning from thence, ſhall have and enjoy all* Liberties *and immunities of* FREE *and naturalSubjects within the dominions of Us, Our Heirs, and Succeſſors, to all intents, conſtructions, aud purpoſes whatſoever, as if they and every of them were born within our realm of* England. I need ſay but little as to this branch of the head further than to obſerve, that the clauſe of the Charter juſt cited, proves clearly, and which cannot be further diſputed, *that all and every of the Subjects, the Inhabitants of* New-England, *which ſhall come to and inhabit within the Province and territory of the ſame, and every of their Children which ſhall happen to be born there, ſhall have and enjoy all the* Liberties,&c. *of* FREE *and naturalSubjects of the realm of* England. Indeed I am ſorry to mention that thisCharter ſhould have been ſo long ſubverted and remained unobſerved by the Publick in ſo intereſting a point, when by timely obſervance it might have ſaved many thouſands from Slavery

very

very that are now dead and mouldered into duft. I hope this eafy found light will not be too late difcovered to direct and fave the prefent Slaves from their Bondage, which many! too many ! groan under : So that I expect the inhabitants of the *American* Provinces will not give any perfon an opportunity of charging them with that infamous character of making or keeping any man or woman Slaves, when they are complaining daily that their Liberties are wrefted from them, and little think how they deprive thefe poor Black People of their Freedom, when there is as little reafon for it as there is for making Slaves of *Britifh* Subjects. The above cited claufe in the Charter, fays, *Thofe born in or fhall come to and dwell within the Province of the* Maffachufetts-Bay are FREE ; from which I am led to think, and which every perfon muft fee, will extend to Black as well as White. But, Reader, excufe me, whoever you are, that may take offence at my conftruing this claufe of the Charter in the manner I have done, it is only my opinion, and every one is at liberty to enjoy his own fentiments upon it as well as I ; therefore I flatter myfelf of hearing foon, that means will be taken by the Legiflature of moft, if not all the Provinces of *North-America,* and the *Weft-India* Iflands,

totally

totally prohibiting the importation of Negroes into the *British* Plantations; and setting at Liberty with univerſal conſent, every Negro throughout the whole, at leaſt in *North-America,* which will be an honour to human nature, to ſay that this great and this only remaining hinderance to the abſolute freedom as well as legality of the *Engliſh* trade is now happily and glorioully aboliſhed; and then we may all cry with ſhouts of joy ! which few more countries in the four quarters of the globe can, *That complete* FREEDOM *both in people and trade is allowed throughout the* Britiſh *Iſlands and Plantations in* America *and the* Weſt-Indies *!*

THE IIId General Head propoſed was, To ſhew the diſadvantages ariſing from this baſe Trade. This head I propoſe to conſider ſeparately, and ſhall 1ſt. Shew the diſadvantages to *Africa* in taking ſo many of its natives away yearly. 2d. Treat of the hurt and prejudice of this Trade with *Europe.* 3d. Shew the diſadvantages to the *Britiſh* Plantations in *America,* particularly to the *Weſt-Indies,* in carrying Black People thither.

The firſt part of this head is, To ſhew the diſadvantages to *Africa* in taking ſo many of its natives yearly. Before I enter upon this branch it may not be improper to mention

tion a few obfervations which Mr. *Pof-tlethwayt* makes upon the great qualities which this country abound with. "Its fituation for commerce is certainly beyond any of the other quarters of the world, for it ftands in the center between the other three, and has thereby a much nearer communication with *Europe*, *Afia*, and *America*, than any other quarter has with the reft. It is wonderfully accommodated for commerce by the interpofion of iflands, and more particularly by the affiftance of the trade winds, which render the navigation fafe, eafy, and conftant. It is furnifhed with the greateft and moft convenient navigable rivers, and perhaps with as many of them as any other of the chief parts of the world : Such are the *Nile*, *Nubia*, *Niger*, *Natal*, which are rivers of the firft magnitude ; befides thefe there are innumerable others, though not equal to the former, are yet very excellent ftreams, fituated for navigation and commerce, and which by their noble courfes penetrate far inland ; if the *Europeans*, &c. would cultivate a human and Chriftian like commerce with the *Africans*, they might through thefe rivers become the medium of an endlefs beneficial commerce. The country is populous beyond credibi-
lity

lity, the soil fruitful, the season for the greatest part mild and clement, and the air salubrious." I must stop in the midst of this agreeable description, being afraid of leading myself into an undue length in this narrative of the beautious perfection of that rich and fruitful part of the world.

I SHALL now consider the disadvantages to *Africa* in taking so many of its natives away yearly. But it is needless to speak much on this head, as most of my Readers will perceive the prejudices to *Africa* in thus draining it of the inhabitants yearly in the manner *Britain* and the Plantations do. I shall mention a few of them. 1st. There can be no loss to any country (particularly to one like *Africa* that is yet mostly to cultivate) equal to that of depopulating it. 2d. It prevents the inland country, where the incessant broils are carried on, from defending themselves against the attacks and encroachments made on their properties by the Kings and Chiefs, whereby many thousands of their subjects being taken prisoners, are sold to the Coasters, they being nourished and caressed by the *Europeans,* particularly by *Britain* and the Colonies, in doing so, for the sake of the Slave Trade to *America,* and the *West-Indies* ; and further, in consequence of this depriving
them

them of defending themſelves againſt theſe baſe aſſaults, it prevents them entirely from cultivating and manuring that fruitful and rich country, to the degree it is capable of. 3d. It ever obſtructs the civilizing of thoſe people, and conſequently of propagating amongſt them the Chriſtian religion, and extending the Trade into the bowels of *Africa*, which by contrary means might be eaſily practicable. 4th. That whilſt the ſlaving Trade of thoſe people, continue to be the great object of the powers that trade there it is to be feared it will ever, as it does at preſent ſpirit up wars and hoſtilities amongſt the Negro Princes and Chiefs, for the ſake of making captives of each other for ſale. And 5th. The greateſt diſadvantage to *Africa*, by thus draining it of the inhabitants is, that it prevents them from cultivating and peopling that great fertile country, of introducing *European* arts and ſciences amongſt them, and of carrying on a friendly, civil, and chriſtian Commerce with them into the heart of their region.

The ſecond branch alluding to the third head was, to treat of the prejudice to *Africa*, and its trade with *Europe*. It is an abſolute fact, that theſe people are inceſſently at war with their neighbouring

Princes

Princes so that they cannot get their busi-
ness looked into or followed, and confequently a great hinderance to the manu-
facturing such quantities of their country's
produce of every kind, to send to *Europe* and
America, *&c.* as they might do, were this
Slave Trade abolished, and the Rulers in
amity, friendship, and concord, one with
another.

It is further a hurt to the *African* trade
with *Europe*, for the Slave Trade has so
gained upon the minds of those men that
traffick to *Africa*, that they never once
think of the other commodities, at least in
such quantities as *Europe* might confume
were the attention neceffary paid to it by
making this the only object of the traders notice, I believe it would turn out
much more profitable to keep wholly
to the produce of this country, *viz.*
gums, ivory, gold and filver duft, *&c.* and
to refign that bafe unchriftian Trade of
Man-felling.

Laftly, on this head, To fhew the difadvantages to the *British* Plantations in *America*, *&c.* in bringing Black people into
them. This will be made very eafily appear when you confider, that thefe numerous Black People, which are yearly brought
into

into the southern-moft parts of *North Ame-rica* and the *Weft-Indies* were very poor at that time, not having a penny to command, and never fo much as once in their lifetime had it in their power to make one half that fum for themfelves, fo that the different Provinces in the Continent, and the Iflands in the *Weft-Indies* are filled with thefe necef-fitous Black People, and muft be put upon the townfhips to which they belong, in cafe this enflaving them be ever abolifhed, which I flatter myfelf, and I hope not vainly, will be done in time, and that with effect. Further, why do they fill their Plantations with Black People, fo unnatural to the Whites, the Proprietors of the different Colonies, when it feems no way difficult to obtain White People to ferve free in their ftead ? *Europe* in general affords numbers of poor and diftreffed objects for that pur-pofe, and if thefe were not overworked, as the Negroes generally are, they would make as good Servants for the *Ame-rican* and *Weft-India* Plantations as the Blacks do. And if the *Europeans* were up-on a level with regard to the price of labour, in their Colonies, I cannot but think they would reap great advantage in laying afide the Slave Trade, and cultivate a friendly and civilized Commerce with the *Africans*.

Until

Until this is done it does not feem poffible that the inland trade of that country fhould ever be extended to the degree it is capable of ; for while the fpirit of *Butchery* and making Slaves of each other, is promoted by the *Europeans, Americans, &c.* amongft thofe people, they will never be able to travel with fafety into the heart of the country, or to cement fuch commercial friendfhip and alliance with them, as will actually introduce our arts and manufactures.

The IVth General Head was, To fhew the advantages arifing from abolifhing this bafe cuftom. This Head I propofe dividing into two parts, 1ft. The advantages to *Africa,* and 2d. The advantages to *Europe* particularly to *Britain* and the Plantations in *America* and the *Weft-Indies.*

First to *Africa.* The advantages that would arife to it, in abolifhing this bafe and unchriftian-like Commerce are numerous, fome of which may be comprehended under the following. 1ft. The abolifhing this Trade may be a means of peopling this country, and of cultivating it in the fame manner with any other country in *Europe* or *Afia,* fo as to render it capable of bearing in as great abundance as the *Eaft-Indies,* fpices of equal quality to thofe

of

of *Banda*, *Ternate*, and *Amboyna* ; I fay, the like fpices might be produced on the rich and fruitful fhores of *Melinda* on the eaft fide, or of the flave coaft on the weft fide of *Africa*, and that as eafy and to as great advantage, as where they are now raifed; the latitude being the fame, and foil not unlike ; and, in fhort, cinnamon and all others, the production of *Eaft* and *Weft-Indies*, by proper management might be raifed here as well as in thofe parts. 2d. It would introduce the Chriftian religion among them, which is a fhame to thefe nations who pretend to hold faft the principles of Chriftianity, to keep fo long hid, and of confequence, be a means of bringing among them the more civilized arts and fciences. 3d. It will recommend the *European* drefs, and introduce their cuftoms among the natives, and of courfe civilize them like other Chriftian nations. Laftly. It will be a means of bringing this country to as great perfection in trade, riches, and grandeur, as any in *Europe*, it being a much more fertile and plentious foil for many valuable productions.

MUCH more could I fay upon the numerous advantages arifing to this excellent country : But let what has been faid fuffice, I leave the reft to the Reader's own feeling

feeling, if he has any for this poor diftreffed *Africa* which groans under a heavy load
of oppreffion.

THE next thing in courfe is, the advantages that would arife to *Europe* in thus
carrying on a Chriftian-like Commerce with
Africa. This trade even in its prefent ftate,
excluding that of the Slaves, is as advan-
tageous as any that is now followed ;
and what will it be when a friendly traffick is carried on ? It is as it were all
profit, the firft coft being fome things of
European, particularly of *Britifh* manufactures, and others generally purchafed with
them ; for which there is in return, gold,
elephant's-teeth, wax, gums, cotton-wool,
divers dying-woods, and Slaves : But this
laft piece of Commerce, *viz.* Man-flaving,
I am far from making a part of the *Britifh*
trade, and I dare fay every humane perfon will be like minded. Thefe are articles
which the country abound in, and would
be ftill cheaper to an immenfe degree, were
the inland parts fettled with their own people ; but inftead of that, a hundred thoufand are yearly carried away. *Britain* pays
but little for the commodities it exports
to *Africa,* being moftly, as obferved before,
its own produce, fuch as worfted and con-
ton cloths of all kinds, brafs, iron, and cop-
per

per work of every fort, particularly large
quantities of all kinds of defenfive arms,
with powder and fhot in proportion ; *Eaft-
India* goods, every kind of *Britifh* manufactures, and a good deal of *American* and
Weft-India rum, &c. It is not eafy to fay
what vaft quantities of the above *Britifh*
and *American* productions would be ex-
haufted yearly among fo great a people,
and in fo very extenfive a country, were the
Slave Trade ftopped. It is the intereft of
every Merchant in *Britain* and the Plantations
who are now concerned in traffick to *Africa,*
to cultivate the inland commerce in its
utmoft extent, as having no manner of concern with the Slave Trade, there being the
greateft reafon to believe, that where they
now export twenty fhillings worth of commodities thither, they would then export
an hundred pound ; and I am inclined to
think when the trade comes to be extended to the degree it will admit of, notwithftanding thofe goods that are imported from
*Africa,*there will ftill be difcovered an infinite variety of trafficable articles, with which
the prefent Traders are totally unacquaint-
ed, and this Trade become the moft beneficial to *Britain, America,* and the *Weft-
Indies,* of any that is at prefent on foot, as
it is common to every individual, and of
which

which the government has taken much notice, by granting an annual fum of ten thoufand pounds fterling for the maintaining and upholding the forts and caftles in the *Britiſh* Settlements in *Africa*, fo that they are entirely defended againft the attacks of any enemy, and their Trade and Colonies fecured by irrefiftible ftrength of forts and caftles.

A GREAT deal more could be mentioned on the thoufands of advantages that may arife to the intereft of *Britain* and the Plantations in abolifhing this wicked Trade : However, I fhall detain my Readers no longer on this head, but as propofed,

CONCLUDE the whole with fome fhort admonitions to thofe concerned, and a method to put this Trade to *Africa* upon a juft and lawful footing. I advife every Merchant and Shipmafter who is in this Trade of Man-flaving to renounce and give it up. What arguments or reafon, pray, can be advanced for his juftification, when he fees fuch threats and curfes againft him, particularly mentioned in the firft head ? Why fhould any perfon incur the penalties of GOD's Law fo daringly for the fake of gain ? Should they think themfelves on a death-bed, what agonies and troubles of mind muft they undergo in the thoughts

thoughts of enflaving fo many miferable creatures, of murdering fo many thoufands of innocent people in the wars they occafion, treacheroufly taking them out of their own country, ufing them barbaroufly, maffacring numbers of them in all the cruel ways imaginable on the paffage, felling them for life, and depriving them even of a comfortable living, notwithftanding they ferve for nothing elfe ; furely the judgment of GOD muft come upon fuch men who will thus ufe their own Brethren who were born to inherit the fame falvation with us, and if his judgment does not come upon them, it will purfue their children unto the third and fourth generation, until the riches that have been thus fcandaloufly amaffed be fquandered away, and they become as poor as thefe Negroes themfelves, by felling of whom fuch unjuft gain was made. But this is only one way out of thoufands that GOD chufes to afflict his enemies in this world. And,

STILL purfuing, that GOD will be revenged on thofe that punifh wrongfully fuch poor Negroes, I fhall infert what the above mentioned Mr. *George Whitefield* fays in a letter to the inhabitants of *Virginia*, &c. " We have," fays he, " a remarkable inftance of GOD's taking
cognizance

" cognizance of, and avenging the quarrel of
" poor Slaves, 2 *Sam.* xxi. 1. There was a
" famine in the days of *David*, three years,
" year after year, and *David* enquired of
" the LORD, and the LORD anſwered, it
" is for *Saul*, and his bloody houſe, becauſe
" he ſlew the *Gibeonites.* Two things are
" here very remarkable, 1ſt. Theſe *Gibe-*
" *onites* were only hewers of wood and
" drawers of water ; or in other words,
" Slaves like yours. 2d. That this plague
" was ſent by GOD *many years after the in-*
" *jury* (the cauſe of the plague) was com-
" mitted. And for what end were this and
" ſuch like examples recorded in holy
" Scripture ? Without doubt for our learn-
" ing. For GOD is the ſame to-day as he
" was yeſterday, and will continue the ſame
" for ever. He does not rejeét the prayer
" of the poor and deſtitute, nor diſregard
" the cry of the meaneſt Negro." When
ſpeaking of the oppreſſion and unchriſtian
uſage theſe poor Negroes meet with from the
Shipmaſters in their paſſage, and from the
Maſters they are ſold to in the ſouth parts
of *America* and the *Weſt-Indies*, he adds,
" The blood of the Negroes ſpilt for theſe
" many years in your reſpeétive Provinces
" will riſe up to Heaven againſt you," together with that loſt in *Africa*, occaſioned by the
Traders

Traders that go thither. It may not
be improper to obferve here, that this
plague was fent by GOD on *Saul* and
his bloody houfe *many years after the
flaughter of the* Gibeonites ; fo may thefe
men reafonably expect, that have occafion-
ed and ftill continue to be the caufe of fpil-
ling fo much innocent blood in *Africa* and
the different Provinces, to have a plague or
curfe come upon them, *many years after the
perpetrating thefe wicked deeds.*

I WILL infert a few queftions, for which
I am indebted to Mr. *Poftlethwayt,* by way
of argument or perfuafion to give up this
enflaving of Men to thofe people who will
be ready to defend this fcandalous Trade to
Africa, and of keeping thefe people in ig-
norance, who are brought into a country
where the gofpel is preached on all fides of
them.

1ft. "WHETHER the people of this country
notwithftanding their colour, are not capable of being civilized and brought into the
Chriftian religion, as well as great numbers
of the *Indians* of *America* and *Afia* have
been ; and whether the primitive inhabitants of all countries fo far as we have been
able to trace them were not once as fa-

H   vage

vage and inhuman as the people in *Africa*, and whether the ancient *Britons* themfelves of our country were not once upon a level with the *Africans* ?

2d. "WHETHER therefore, there is not a probability that thofe people might in time, by proper management in the *Europeans*, become as wife, as induftrious, as humane, and as good Chriftians, as the people of any other country ?

3d. "WHETHER their rational faculties are not in general equal to thofe of any other of the human fpecies ; and whether they are not, from experience, as capable for mechanical and manufactural arts and trades, as even the Bulk of the *Europeans* ?

4th. "WHETHER it would not bemore to the intereft of all the *European* Nations concerned in the Trade to *Africa*, rather to endeavour to cultivate a friendly and humane Commerce with thefe people, into the very centure of their extended country, than to content themfelves only with fkimming a trifling portion of Trade upon the Coaft of *Africa* ?

5th. "WHETHER the greateft hinderance and obftruction to the *European*'s cultivating

ting a Chriftian-like and humane Commerce with thofe populous countries has not wholly proceeded from that unjuft Traffick called the Slave Trade, which is carried on by the *Europeans Americans, &c.*

6th. " WHETHER thisTrade and this only was not the primary caufe, and ftill continues to be the chief caufe of thefe eternal and inceffant broils, quarrels,and animofities which fubfift between the Negro Princes and Chiefs ; and confequently- of thofe endlefs wars which abide among them, and which they are induced to carry on in order to make prifoners of one another for the fake of the Slave Trade ?

7th. " WHETHER,if trade was carried on with them for a feries of years,as it has been with moft other favage countries, and the *Europeans* gave no incouragement whatever to the Slave Trade, thofe cruel wars among the Blacks would not ceafe, and a fair and honourable Commerce in time take place throughout the whole country ?

8th. " WHETHER the example of the *Dutch* in the *Eaft-Indies*, who have civilized innumerable of the natives, and brought them to the *European* way of cloathing, *&c.*

does

does not give reafonable hopes that thefe fuggeftions are not vifionary, but founded on experience as well as on humane and Chriftian principles ?

9th. "WHETHER Commerce in general has not proved the great means of civilizing all nations, even the moft favage and brutal ; and why not the *Africans ?*

10th. "WHETHER the territory of the *European* nations who are interefted in the Colonies and Plantations in *America,* are not populous enough, or may be rendered fo, by proper encouragement given to matrimony and the breed of foundling infants,to fupply their refpective Colonies with labourers in the place of Negro Slaves ? And

Laftly. "WHETHER the *Britifh* dominions in general have not an extent of territory fufficient to increafe and multiply their inhabitants ; and whether it is not their own faults that they do not increafe them fufficiently to fupply their Colonies and Plantations, with Whites inftead of Blacks ?"

I MAKE no doubt, but fome perfons who are concerned in the Slave Trade to *Africa,* will attempt making anfwer to fome of thefe queftions : But I prefume
there

there are others of them they will not venture upon, knowing they are founded upon reafon and truth, and I hope will have great influence on thofe this Treatife concern.

I would add one neceffary query more, to thofe who hold the fword of juftice, and who muft account to God for the ufe they make of it. Since the *Englifh* Law is fo truly valuable for its juftice, how can they overlook the barbarous deaths and wrongful Slavery of the unhappy *Africans*, without trial or proof of being guilty of crimes adequate to their punifhments ? Why are thofe Mafters of veffels (who are not the moft confiderate of men) fuffered to be fovereign arbiters of the lives of thefe miferable Negroes in their paffage, and allowed with impunity to deftroy, may I not fay murder their fellow creatures in a manner fo cruel as can never be related but with fhame and horror ? Anfwer me this, ye pretended Judges and Governors in the different Colonies where fuch practices are ufed, and not be fhocked at the negligence you have fleeped in. Since you are put in remembrance of it now, I hope and fincerely wifh, I, or any other perfon may not have occafion to remind you of the fame again, but that you will punifh with

equity

equity all thofe who import Negroes ; there being hundreds of poor *Europeans* that would be glad to come and ferve in any of the *Britifh* Plantations, and thofe that could not pay a paffage doubtlefs wouid fell part of their time for it ; and this I make no doubt, confidering they have not the charge of their funeral and death-bed expences and fundry other things to pay, will come nigh if not full as cheap as buying and keeping Negroes ; and it will be attended with this advantage, that thefe White people when they have ferved fome years in the loweft capacities turn out upon the wafte land, marry, and in a few years we fee a town well fettled, and in lefs than fifty years there will be an increafe of fourfold ; by this means the country will fill up and we become refpectable and fecure from an enemy, and furnifhed with every conveniency of life. And you Governers, &c. who have the legiflative power in your hands will ftill further make Laws and put them in execution, ftopping any further importation of Slaves into the Provinces or Iflands where you are the Reprefentative head, fo that in that time they may furnifh themfelves with fufficient numbers, and by proper ufage keep up that quantity which fo much decreafe by improper ma-

management. Now give me leave to proceed

In a method to put this Trade to *Africa* on a juft and lawful footing. Firft, in order to this, it is my humble opinion, if I may be allowed to give it, that there be a number of men who may chufe to venture in this Trade, both in *Britain* and theColonies, that fhall be incorporated into feparate bodies by the name of *Englifh*, or *Britifh* ; *American*, or *New England African* companies, or by the denomination of other Provinces in *America*, or Plantations in the *Weft-Indies* ; and thefe companies fhall equip and rig out as many veffels as they think proper, loading them with *Britifh America*, *Eaft* and *Weft-India* goods, and bring back in return, the rich and plentiful produce of *Africa*. But before I go any further into this point it muft be obferved, there is one real hinderance in the way which muft be removed, or elfe no man or company need ever think of penetrating into the heart of this country, but juft content themfelves with taking the fkim of this Trade, leting the body ftand, and that is, the Slave Trade; this muft be entirely renounced and given up by the *Europeans*, particularly by *Britain* and the Colonies ; then

then we may with a good face and confcience travel into the heart of *Africa*, and meet with a friendly and hearty reception from the natives, who will trade with us, and give in exchange their valuable productions for our goods which are generally exported thither.

WHEN that great, that only chief obftacle, the Slave Trade is removed, then *Britain* and the Colonies will flourifh by fo great and profitable a Commerce. Think what a great addition it will make to their traffick, the furnifhing a hundred thoufand people annually, more than are at prefent with cloathing, powder, fhot, and warlike arms, and many more things needlefs here to enumerate out of England ; rum, and fundry other articles out of *America* and the *Weft-Indies*. It is fuppofed that the above extraordinary number of Blacks are taken out of *Africa* yearly, and either murdered or made Slaves of, by the fhips that go there out of *Bofton*, &c. and what advantages may arife to the inhabitants in peopling, and confequently of cultivating and manuring their ground, and of bringing their rich trade to the perfection it is capable of, with *Britain*, &c. is hard to fay, when the innermoft parts of that great and fruitful country is fettled,

and

and a free and happy trade carried into the heart of it : But thus far I will venture to fay, as I have done already, that where twenty fhillings worth of commodities is at prefent exported an hundred pound will be, when a friendly Commerce is carried on with the natives.

THESE companies may fay, that if once this trade is fet on foot, other *European* powers, who have Settlements in *Africa* will invade them whenever they begin to thrive by not having fufficient funds for the keeping in good defence the forts, &c. on the Settlements. As to this I anfwer, that thofe companies have a fum of ten thoufand pounds fterling annually, from the Crown of *Britain,* for maintaining and upholding the forts and caftles that are built upon the *Britifh* Colonies, which with the duties arifing from the Trade will be fufficient to maintain, uphold, and defend them with ftrength fuperior to the ftrongeft enemy.

THUS far I hope I have removed your fears of inability in fupporting and continuing this Trade, and likewife have moved ways and means to put the fame on a juft and lawful footing. Now let me,

I   patient

patient Reader, conclude with a ſhort Ex-
hortation to the Ship-maſters and Merchants concerned in this Trade, in part
of which I have had recourſe again to
my good old Friend Mr. *Benezet*.

I BEG you all would fly from the
oppreſſion and Bondage to which the poor
Africans are ſubjeſted, loofe the bonds
from off their necks, and thereby extri-
cate yourſelves from a cuſtom which is per-
nicious to your welfare here and hereafter ;
and as you are ſenſible moſt men have ob-
jections to this baſe, unlawful Trade, you
ought to vindicate yourſelves to the world,
upon principles of reaſon, honeſty, and humanity, and then you will not attack the
perſons, or invade the rights of theſe people.
I believe thoſe who are concerned in this
Trade will be at a loſs to make this juſtifi-
cation but upon motives ſo weak and un-
reaſonable, that I do not think any of
them which have been advanced for their
defence worthy of notice; and if they are un-
deſerving of that, they certainly are below
regard ; therefore I think *you ſhould forever
lay it aſide.* This is the beſt and ſhorteſt
way ; for *there ſhould be no trade carried
on,* it being a national and provincial concern, *but ſuch as is juſtifiable both to* GOD
and

and man, and this is in direct oppofition to both. But laying man's refentment afide, which is of little moment in comparifon with that of the Almighty's, I counfel you once more to think of a future reckoning, confider what reafons you will be able to produce at the great and laft day. You now accumulate riches and live in pleafure ; but what will you do in the end, and that will be but fhort ? What if you fhould be called hence and hurried out of this world under the vaft load of blood guiltinefs that is now lying on your fouls ? How many thoufands have you been the iftruments to, and primary caufe of being killed in the wars and broils with the *African* Chiefs, wanting to obtain your number to enflave ; and how many have you killed in the paffage, when thefe poor Creatures were trying to retrieve their Liberty which they had in their own country, and which you unjuftly take from them, or rather chufing to die than take food to nourifh and preferve themfelves for being mancipated with their children after them ?

It is declared in the moft exprefs terms in Scripture, that thieves and murderers fhall not inherit the kingdom of God. You who

who are in this Trade take warning by that, and if you have any thoughts or Chriſtian feeling you muſt certainly renounce it ; for that you are thieves and murderers(I hope after what has been ſaid) will not be diſputed ; and you ſhould think that at the ſame time and by the ſame means you are treaſuring up worldly riches, you are treaſuring up fountains of wrath againſt the day of anger and vengeance that ſhall come upon the workers of iniquity, unleſs timely repented of.

WHAT injuſtice is greater ? What offence more heinous ? Is there any carries in it more conſummate guilt than that in which you now live ? How can you lift your culpable eyes to Heaven ? How can you pray for mercy, or hope for favour from him that made and formed you, while you go on thus boldly and publickly diſhonouring him, in degrading and deſtroying the nobleſt workmanſhip of his hands in this ſublunary world ? Can you think that GOD will hear your prayers, receive your ſupplications, or grant your deſires, while you act thus groſſly and openly againſt his divine revealed will and pleaſure ? And do you ſuppoſe that he who is the Parent of all nations, the Protector of

all

all people, and the Father of all men, will not revenge the male-treatment of his off-spring whom he once so loved as to give his only begotten Son, *that whosoever be-lieved in him should not perish, but have ever-lasting life* ? This love of GOD to man, which is disclosed in Scripture, adds double provocation to your crimes ; for if GOD regards us with so much affection, we ought also to esteem one another.

PERMIT yourselves for a moment to re-flect equitably and deliberately upon the nature of this horrid, detestable, vile, and abominable Man Trade, and your hearts must certainly relent, if you have not lost all sense of benevolence, all sympathy and compassion towards those of your Brethren who have the same capacities, understand-ings and souls, and who were born to in-herit the same salvation with you ; I say, if you are not callous to every Christian, hu-mane, and manly sensibility, you certainly must feel compassion for those extremely oppressed people, when you think what miseries, what devastations and massacres among them you have been the author of, and all for filthy lucre's sake. The thoughts of this accursed Trade touches my very heart, and finding if I continue any
-longer

longer I ſhall get out of the bounds of decency, muſt therefore conclude. And if all you have read ſhould have no weight upon your hardned hearts, this remains for my conſolation that I have done my duty; and I pray! Fervently pray! That GOD would have mercy on your ſinful ſouls; and that he of his infinite goodneſs would grant that you may be made ſenſible of your guilt and repent of theſe your execrable and really deteſtable deeds.

F I N I S.

☞ The Author makes no doubt but the Publick, after reading this Pamphlet, will readily agree with him, that the words in the Dedication are verified, " That it was put " together with more good intent than abili-" ty," which he is very ſenſible of : But at the ſame time thinks all criticiſm and ſcrutinizing ſhould be laid aſide, when they reflect, that the will to do good is next in order to the action itſelf.

www.ingramcontent.com/pod-product-compliance
Lightning Source LLC
Chambersburg PA
CBHW021512090426
42739CB00007B/571